INVESTIGATING HISTORY

G000098122

Life in VICTORIAN BRITAIN

Fiona Goodman and Peter Kent

SIMON & SCHUSTER
EDUCATION

First published in 1992 in Great Britain by
Simon & Schuster Education
Campus 400, Maylands Avenue
Hemel Hempstead, Herts HP2 7EZ

Reprinted in 1993

**A catalogue record for this book is
available from the British Library**

ISBN 0-7501-0215-2

Designed by Helen Castle
Illustrated by Peter Kent
Printed in Great Britain by
Dotesios Ltd, Trowbridge, Wiltshire

Contents

General introduction

....

Investigating History is a series of photocopiable resources designed to cover the National Curriculum for History at Key Stage 2. The Programmes of Study are covered through the full range of skills required in the Attainment Targets.

The series offers one book for each History Study Unit. Each book contains a general introduction, an historical introduction, 20 units and a set of Resource sheets. A unit consists of a double-page spread of teacher's notes and a pupils' activity sheet which may be photocopied. Each unit presents stimulating activities which encourage a skills-based investigative approach to History.

Listed below are the Attainment Targets and the outline for the History Core Study Unit 3 - Victorian Britain.

Attainment Targets:
AT1 Knowledge and understanding of history
AT2 Interpretations of history
AT3 The use of historical sources

Core Study Unit 3 Victorian Britain	Units in book
Economic developments	2, 3, 5, 6, 7, 8
Public welfare	9, 10, 12
Religion	11
Scientific and cultural achievements	4, 13, 14, 15
Domestic life	16, 17, 18, 19, 20

USING THE BOOK

The following paragraphs give a brief explanation of how the activity sheets and the different sections in the teacher's notes work.

Activity sheets

In general, the activities are suitable for individual, group or class work. The activity sheets are intended to provide stimuli to both teachers and pupils which may then lead to the development of individual or group historical enquiry. The sheets are not intended to be worked through methodically; teachers will wish to select and adapt the activities and ideas to suit the needs of the children.

The resource sheets at the back of the book are intended to supplement particular activity sheets; indication is given in the teacher's notes if and when a resource sheet may be relevant.

Teacher's notes

- The *Skills* section lists the historical skills which the children will be developing in working on the activity sheet.

- The *National Curriculum* charts only indicate the Attainment Targets which will be studied through working on the activity sheet. Attainment targets covered by extension activities and cross-curricular work are not listed in these charts.

- The *Background information* section gives useful historical information, particularly highlighting some areas with which children may be unfamiliar.

- The *Introductory work* section gives suggestions for pre-experience and ways of introducing the sheets.

- The *Using the sheet* section details any equipment children might need, explains what the children are expected to do and makes suggestions for prompting questions or activities to help them get the most out of the activity sheet.

- The *Extension activities* often include suggestions for cross-curricular activities and ways of developing the skills and knowledge promoted by the activity sheet.

Investigating History should not be seen as the entire scheme of work for a project. Children should also have the opportunity to handle and examine artefacts and original documentation and, if possible, to visit sites and museums which will further enrich their studies. They should also have access to research and information books which will allow them to investigate particular areas of interest.

RESOURCES
Pupil information books

Growing up in Victorian Britain, S Ferguson, Batsford
A Victorian Sunday, J Hughes, Wayland
Victorian Children, E Allen, A and C Black
Two Victorian Families, S Wagstaff, A and C Black
Victorian Children, A Steel, Wayland: 'Beginning History' series
The Victorians, G Thie, Basil Blackwell: 'Living in the past' series
How we used to live: 1851-1901, F Kelsall, Macdonald
How we used to live: Victorians Early and Late, D Evans, A and C Black
Florence Nightingale, Franklin Watts 'Lifetimes' series
A 19th Century Railway Station, F Macdonald and J James, Simon and Schuster

General introduction

The 'Finding out about' series by Batsford includes: *Victorian Childhood; Victorian Country Life; Victorian London; Victorian Schools; Victorian Towns; Victorian Law and Order; Victorian Public Health and Housing*

The 'Into the past' series by Longman includes: *Entertainment and Transport in 1900; At School and in the Country in 1900; At Home and in the Street in 1900*

The 'Life and times' series by Wayland includes: *Dickens and the Victorians; Stephenson and the Industrial Revolution*

The 'Great Lives' series by Wayland includes: *Queen Victoria* and *Florence Nightingale*

Teacher's information

Teacher's reference books

Victorian Times, P Noble and J Lawrie, Unwin Hyman (a photocopiable resource book)

In Search of History 1714-1900, J F Aylett, Edward Arnold

Developing Britain 1740-1900, J Nichol, Basil Blackwell

Victorian Cities, A Briggs, Penguin

Victorian People, A Briggs, University of Chicago Press

The English Terraced House, S Muthesius, Yale University Press

Victorian Architecture, R Dixon and S Muthesius, Thames and Hudson

For Queen and Country: Britain in the Victorian Age, M Drabble, Andre Deutsche

Victorian Architecture, R J Furneaux, Penguin

Victorian Comfort: a social history of design 1830-1900, J Gloag, David and Charles

How They Were Taught, P H J H Gosden, Basil Blackwell

English Life in the Nineteenth Century, R Hart, Putnam's

The Seaside Holiday, A Hern

The Great Exhibition of 1851: A Commemorative Album, HMSO

Victorians at Home, S Lasdun, Weidenfeld and Nicolson

Victoria R I, E Longford, Weidenfeld and Nicolson

Leisure and Pleasure in the Nineteenth Centry, S Margetson

The Victorian House, J Marshal and I Willox, Sidgwick and Jackson

Sixty Years a Queen, Sir Herbert Maxwell, Harmsworth

London Labour and the London Poor, H Mayhew, Spring Books

Human Documents of the Victorian Golden Age, R Pyke

Brunel and his World, J Pudney, Thames and Hudson

A History of Everyday Things in England, M and P Quennel

London's Underworld, P Quennel, Hamlyn

Victorian Engineering, L T C Rolt, Penguin, 1974

The Private Life of the Queen, E Sheffield, Gresham Books

Florence Nightingale, C W Smith, Constable

Queen Victoria: her life and times, C W Smith, Hamish Hamilton

Victorian England (Life in England 5) W Stobbs and A Williams-Ellis, Blackie

Queen Victoria, L Strachey, Collins

Endangered Lives: Public Health in Victorian Britain, A Wohl, Dent

Contempory periodicals (good for pictures)

The Graphic

The Illustrated London News

Punch

Historical fiction

The Railway Children, E Nesbit

Tom's Midnight Garden, P Pearce

The Peppermint Pig, N Bawden

Little Women/Good Wives, Louisa M Alcott

Alice in Wonderland, Lewis Caroll

Lark Rise to Candleford, Flora Thompson

David Copperfield, Charles Dickens

Oliver Twist, Charles Dickens

The Bonnie Pit Laddie, Frederick Grice

A likely lad, Gillian Avery

Ride the Iron Horse, Marjorie Darke

The Stove Haunting, B Mooney

Posters

Pictorial Charts offer the following posters: *Age of Expansion; Age of Expansion - Evidence in Pictures; How we used to live - Early Victorians; How we used to live - Late Victorians; Victorian homes; Canals; Railways; Town life in Mid-Victorian England.*

Useful addresses/Places to visit

English Heritage Education Service, Keysign House, 429 Oxford Street, London W1R 2HD

Ironbridge Gorge Museum, Telford

Beamish Open Air Museum, Durham

Black Country Industrial Museum, Dudley

Armley Mill Industrial Museum, Leeds

Railway Museum, York

Castle Museum, York

Royalty and Empire Exhibition, Windsor

Osborne House, Isle of Wight (English Heritage)

The Museum of Childhood, Edinburgh

The Museum of London, London EC2

Museum of Childhood, Bethnal Green, London E2

The London Toy and Model Museum, London

The Victoria and Albert Museum, London

The Museum of Costume, Bath

Doll Museum, Warwick

Historical introduction

Alexandrina Victoria, the niece of William IV, came to the throne upon his death in 1837, when she was only 18 years old. The succession of this slight, retiring girl, the first queen to rule in her own right since Anne, was as complete a change as was possible to imagine from the dissolute and profligate sons of George III. If only in the person of the Queen, the reign of Victoria (she fortunately abandoned her first name – Alexandrinian does not make a very convincing adjective) was to be very different from any before. It was to be distinguished above all by sheer length: Victoria died in 1901 and so was queen for over 64 years, the longest reign in British history. She presided over the unprecedented changes of the 19th century when the country doubled its population, trebled its wealth and completed the transformation from a largely rural society to an overwhelmingly industrial and urban one.

No other monarch had the opportunity for so many 'firsts' as Victoria, who ruled during arguably the most inventive and innovative period in British history. She was the first sovereign to travel by train, to use the telephone, to be photographed, to be filmed, to have her voice recorded, to see by electric light and to have an anaesthetic; if she had cared to she could have been the first to travel in the air and under the sea. Victoria was also the first British monarch to reign over a democracy where most adult males could vote by secret ballot, where education was compulsory and trade unions were legal and largely respectable.

As well as the onrush of technological and constitutional innovation there was an equally vigorous expansion of industry, trade and empire. Victoria presided over the largest empire in history: no other ruler has had so many subjects of so many different races and creeds. Her navy was the largest and most powerful in the history of the world and her country increased in population and wealth with every year.

Unlike emperors of the past, Victoria had no absolute authority; her main contribution was to lend her name to this extraordinarily energetic period in the history of Britain. But so complex and various were the facets of Britain during her reign that the adjective 'Victorian' must be extremely general in its application. Victorian architecture encompassed austere reproductions of ancient Greek temples, the most exhuberant of Gothic fantasies and the first truly modern buildings of glass, steel and concrete. The literary world of the 1830s and 40s, of the early Dickens and Thackeray, had very little in common with the end of the century, with Oscar Wilde, Aubrey Beardsley and their mannered aestheticism.

The vital point to remember about Victorians is that they were living in an age of accelerating change. It is rather difficult to accept this when we look at their photographs: the men solemn, bewhiskered and girdled with watch chains, the women draped with voluminous swathes of material. We tend, too, to think of Victorian buildings as being dark, solid and gloomy. Yet this is a perception gained through looking at black-and-white photographs and at buildings covered with a hundred years of soot. Look instead at a painting by Frith or Dyce, or some newly-scrubbed brickwork at a railway station, to gain an impression of how colourful their world really was. Victorian cities were raw and new, the bricks red and yellow, the slates shiny and uniformly grey. In the streets there were brightly-painted carts and omnibuses. People's clothes were coloured with new artificial chemical dyes, often in garish hues.

It is worth stressing how new Victorian England was at the end of the nineteenth century. Virtually every major public building and institution, nearly every suburb and the whole railway network were less than 50 years old. To an MP in 1891 the Houses of Parliament, completed in 1854, was a modern building, as up-to-date as the Festival Hall is to us. The vast hospitals and asylums that then loomed outside every city were in most cases less than 30 years old. The board and elementary schools were, in virtually all cases, newer for the child of 1891 than the mobile classroom in the corner of the playground is for the child of today. The railway network was still not complete in 1891, and to give some idea of its novelty St Pancras Station, the very cathedral of Victorian railways, was newer for the traveller of 1891 than Heathrow Airport is for us. Remnants of the older world were giving way on all fronts to the new, which held no terrors for the Victorians. Most of them embraced the future with unbounded enthusiasm, always confident of their ability to improve on the past.

The Victorian Age has three distinct phases. The first ended in the mid-1850s when the process of constructing the iron, coal and cotton industries and much of the basic railway network was completed. Britain dominated the world markets in a way that was never to be seen again. Nothing symbolises this period more aptly than the Great Exhibition of 1851, when a dazzling array of invention and ingenuity, most of it British, was displayed in the most technically original building since the medieval cathedrals.

The second phase, from about 1860 to 1880, can be seen as one of consolidation and exploitation of the wealth created during the previous decades. it was then that Britain's towns and cities were transformed, when most of the nation's town halls and museums were built, when vast works of civic improvement were undertaken to remedy the evils of chaotic urban expansion. Schools, churches, colleges and hospitals were built in their thousands; parks and

Historical introduction

cemeteries were provided on a lavish scale; and sewer building became something of a national obsession explicable only to people who lived close to fetid cesspits.

Having acquired such enormous wealth it was only natural that the Victorians would devote more energy to spending it rather than accumulating more. From about 1890 industrial and commercial complacency slowly led to a relative decline in Britain's fortunes. Although Britain seemed at the zenith of its power at Victoria's Golden Jubilee in 1897, with a vast empire, 30 miles of warships anchored in the Solent and apparently inexhaustible wealth, it was losing ground in the crucial areas of industrial innovation. The new industries concerned with chemicals and electricity were stronger in Germany; America was leading the world in the design and manufacture of machine tools, the backbone of a truly modern economy. Britain retained its primacy only in industries past their peak. Significantly, the early electric tube railways under London – another first for Britain – were largely financed by an American and equipped with trains shipped from across the Atlantic. Merchants and traders concentrated more on the territories of the growing empire while foreign competition began to erode the supremacy of British goods in the Far East and America.

Victoria herself went through transformations similar to her country's. From the modest girl queen of the 1840s – such a welcome change from her repulsive uncles – she progressed to being the model and mirror of respectable family life with her beloved Albert and nine children. After Albert's death from typhoid in 1861 (the drains were to blame) she went from a period of being the generally detested reclusive Widow of Windsor to an Indian summer of popular acclaim as the Mother of Empire, whose statue could be found in every clime and continent and after whom countless little girls, numerous railways stations, several colonial capitals and an ill-fated battleship were named. (The unfortunate *HMS Victoria* was rammed on manoeuvres by a companion and sank.) Victoria was the living embodiment of the principle that all one has to do to become popular is to live long enough. There had been a strong republican movement in the 1860s but by 1897 this had evaporated, to be replaced by clouds of uncritical adulation. Sir Herbert Maxwell, MP, spoke for millions of true Britons when he sighed, 'Thank Heaven that throughout this critical period of change we have remained the subjects of Victoria the Great and Good.'

Reality, of course, was rather different. For every glittering success of the period there was a grim human cost. Much of the population lived in jerry-built towns around the factories. It was not until the 1890s that concerted municipal efforts began to provide better housing. Although the combined efforts of growing trade union power and philanthropically-inspired legislation removed the worst horrors of factory life, and compulsory elementary education largely stopped child labour, the conditions of the unskilled working classes remained dreadful.

Most large towns and cities still have their quota of solemn statues of Victorian philanthropists, commemorating their efforts to improve the position of the less fortunate. The government hardly concerned itself with social issues; most of the laws that attempted to deal with the conditions of the working classes were the results of the labours of concerned individuals like Lord Shaftesbury. It is perhaps not surprising that, just as the wealth of the country, and much of the misery attendant on its production, was the result of free enterprise, so, too, should be social reform. Promoting this concern were mainly moral precepts, but there was also a degree of political self-interest. The middle and upper classes were tiny in proportion to the mass of the working population and were terrified of their revolutionary potential. If the middle classes sympathised with the labourers in their reasonable demands, it might give them power to curtail less reasonable ones.

Looking back on Victorian society it seems solid and immutable but the 'respectable' middle-class Victorians themselves knew the swirling forces beneath them and just how precarious their social fabric was. (Victorian builders, too, knew that the villas they sold to the aspiring often had foundations only a couple of bricks thick – in one case, a layer of crushed ginger-beer bottles!)

The political history of Victorian Britain is largely a story of how the pressures from below were contained and absorbed with great success – except for the situation in Ireland. When Victoria came to the throne only about five per cent of all adults, about 12 per cent of all men, could vote and the rural areas were still over-represented in Parliament. Only five years before she became queen the Reform Act of 1832 had removed some of the more ludicrous anomalies such as that of Old Sarum, a hillside outside Salisbury populated only by sheep, which sent two MPs to Westminster when large industrial towns like Manchester and Bolton had none.

Politics were dominated by two great parties, the Whigs and the Tories. When Victoria came to the throne they hardly differed in social and economic matters, except that the Whigs were less inclined to give unqualified support to the crown, the aristocracy and the Anglican Church. During the first half of Victoria's reign, the Whigs and Tories slowly began to transform themselves into two recognisably different modern political parties, the Liberals and the Conservatives.

Historical introduction

In the 1840s these two parties seemed to have no relevance at all for the working classes who could neither join nor vote for them and whose interests were worlds away from the landed gentry who mainly sat in the House of Commons. Economic problems caused real hardship during the 40s – not for nothing was the decade known as the 'Hungry 40s' – and this stimulated a mass movement known as the Chartists. The Chartists wanted what many now think of as entirely sensible reforms which they set out in the People's Charter. There were six points: every man should have the vote, the ballot should be secret, there should be equal electoral districts, there should be no qualification of owning property for MPs, who should be paid, and parliament should be elected annually. In 1848, the year in which revolutions shook the thrones of Europe, the Chartists marched on the Houses of Parliament with a monster petition containing three million names. The Government was seriously alarmed; the Duke of Wellington took charge of its defence. Ten thousand troops were stationed at strategic points, 200,000 special constables were sworn in, government offices were garrisoned with clerks and workmen, and all over London the shutters went up in the grand houses. But England was not Europe; revolutions were things that happened elsewhere. It rained on the Chartist rally and when the great petition was delivered to Parliament in a cab it was found to have been signed by Queen Victoria, the Duke of Wellington and General Tom Thumb, so nobody took it very seriously.

The impetus for reform that motivated the Chartists then passed to the two main parties. Despite the greater radical propensities of the Liberals, it was Disraeli's Conservative government that introduced the Reform Act of 1867. This gave the vote to all men aged over 21 who were either householders or lodgers paying a rent of at least £10 a year, and doubled the electorate to about two million. The secret ballot was introduced in 1872 by Gladstone's Liberal government, who also introduced the Third Reform Act of 1884 which gave the vote to virtually all men who were householders. Women could still not vote, and the Queen thoroughly approved of this. With most of the working class now able to vote, the two parties had to pay serious attention to their demands.

The main differences between Conservatives and Liberals were in foreign policy. Disraeli's party was bent on expanding Britain's overseas interests – it was he who gained control of the Suez Canal and proclaimed Victoria Empress of India – while the Liberals were committed to free trade, financial economy and political reform. But however much he protested, Gladstone was powerless to stop Britain acquiring very large parts of Africa and the Far East, nor could he disentangle Britain from Ireland.

In some ways Britain acquired much of its empire haphazardly. British traders penetrated ever more remote areas of the world and, to protect their interests, the government assumed political control. Because of this the British army was almost continually engaged in a series of small but fierce wars. The Chinese, Sikhs, Maoris, Matabeles, Zulus, Dervishes and Afghans were all brought to battle, with virtually inevitable results, '... for we have got, the Gatling gun and they have not'. Britain's most precious possession was India, and the aim of much of Britain's foreign policy was to protect the sea route to the east.

Britain's involvement in the Crimean War resulted from an alliance with Turkey and France, aimed at denying the Russian fleet access to the Mediterranean where it could disrupt British shipping. This was a bungled affair, notable only for the heroic folly of the charge of the Light Brigade and the lethal incompetence of the medical services which gave Florence Nightingale her opportunity. The other major war of Victoria's reign was fought in South Africa against the two independent Boer states of the Transvaal and the Orange Free Strate, the issue being control of their gold and diamond mines, in which there were heavy investments and a large workforce from the British Empire. The British army found it difficult to subdue the Boers and the war was still dragging on when Victoria died.

She was interred beside Albert in the royal mausoleum at Frogmore, ending the extraordinary period to which she gave her name. It had been a time of headlong change and extreme paradox. While Tennyson or Browning seem to be the authentic Victorian poetic voice, remember that Gerard Manley Hopkins was also writing in her reign. 'The Yellow Book' and *fin de siècle* decadence was Victorian, as well as Shakespeare with the naughty bits expunged and the strange practice of covering up table legs. The Victorians idolised children, in fact they almost invented the concept of childhood, and yet they were quite happy to exempt ten-year-olds from school if they had to work to support their parents. The Victorians probably built more churches than all the other ages put together yet only 35 per cent of them attended, and while Victorian clerics preached, Victorian scientists and philosophers were equally busy making discoveries and speculations that undermined the foundations of religious certainty. Victorians were keen on faith but also wracked with doubt. In short, it is almost impossible to point to anything that is typical of the period. If it happened between 1837 and 1901 then it is 'Victorian', but apart from this basic commonality the distinguishing features of the age are, above all, energy and inventiveness. Victorians DID things; and most of us still live, work, pray, are educated or healed in, or travel on, at least one of their creations.

Activity Sheets and Teacher's Notes

1 Victoria the record breaker Teacher's notes

Skills

Chronological ordering
Making a timeline
Analysing different aspects of change

Attainment Targets

Level	AT1	AT2	AT3
2			
3	✓		✓
4	✓		✓
5			

Background information

Victoria became queen when she was 18 years old, after the death of her uncle, William IV in 1837. She married her German cousin, Albert, in 1839 and they had nine children, five boys and four girls. For further details of Victoria and her family, see *Resource sheet 1* (which shows her family tree) and the *Historical introduction* on page 6.

Introductory work

You might begin by asking the children if they know of any streets, buildings, statues etc named after Queen Victoria or her husband Albert. A lot of towns have a 'Victoria Road' or a statue of Victoria. London is full of reminders of Victoria's reign – Victoria Station, Victoria Coach Station, The Victoria and Albert Museum and the Royal Albert Hall.

It might also be useful to set Victorian times in a time perspective. You could use the royal family tree on *Resource sheet 1* to trace our royal family back to Victorian times, or make a timeline. (An unravelled toilet roll with each sheet representing 10 years is quite effective, or you could fix a string across the classroom and peg on important dates and events.)

Using the sheet

The children will need to put the dates in chronological order first. They could either cut them out and arrange them, or write them out. If the children have not drawn a timeline before you will need to go through this skill with them. After the dates are put on the line the events could be illustrated; any other dates or events met during the topic can be added later. Children could use the timeline to locate dates and measure periods of time, eg: Can you work out how long Victoria reigned?

Extension activities

1 You could encourage children to discuss why Victoria was the first monarch to do all these things. The main point to be brought out is that Victorian times were a period of great progress and change; the children will find out more about this as the topic progresses. Although we may find the things on the sheet commonplace they would have been thought impossible or certainly very strange at the beginning of Victoria's reign.

At the end of the topic the children might refer back to this introductory sheet and try to think of reasons why so much change did take place.

2 *Resource Sheet 1* can be used for work on Victoria's family tree, eg Can the children work out what relation Elizabeth II is to Queen Victoria? How many kings and queens were there between Victoria and our Queen? What can the children find out about royal first names?

3 Children could compare our Queen with Queen Victoria. What might our Queen have been the 'first monarch' to do? Children could research more comparisons, eg clothes, lifestyle, size of family, importance etc.

Queen Victoria reigned for longer than any other British monarch. She was the first queen or king to do many things that we take for granted.

to be photographed

1837

1844 ①

to be filmed

1896 ①

to have her voice recorded

1888 ①

1901

to be lit by electric light

1885 ①

to have an anaesthetic

1853 ①

to use the telephone

1886 ①

She was also the first queen to travel by train:

We arrived yesterday morning having come from Windsor, in half an hour, free from dust and crowds and heat. I am quite charmed by it.

What did Victoria like about the train?

Draw a timeline for Victoria's reign. Put the date of each 'first' on it.

2 The factory system

Skills

Empathising with people in the past
Analysing cause and effect
Analysing changes over a period of time

Attainment targets

Level	AT1	AT2	AT3
2	✓		
3	✓		
4	✓		
5			

Background information

During the early part of the 18th century most goods were made by hand in people's homes – this was called cottage industry or the domestic system. As demand for products such as cloth grew, machines were invented to speed up the process of production and factories were built to house them. This was the beginning of the Industrial Revolution. The invention of the steam engine further expanded the factory system.

Large factories were built by rich manufacturers. Many country people flocked to work in the ever-growing towns. The town portrayed on sheet 9 *Public health* gives a picture of the living conditions many found; working conditions also proved to be arduous and boring. Factories had strict rules and workers were watched by stern overseers.

Introductory work

The teacher might go through the history of the Industrial Revolution, identifying some of its causes and the effects on the cottage industries and domestic workers. Children might select from a list of causes which they think was the most important reason for the decline of the domestic system and the rise of factories.

Using the sheet

The sheet asks the children to say whether they think the factory system was a good or bad thing for the people. In addition to this they might say how it would have affected each of the people. The main points to bring out about each picture are the following:
* *Home nail worker* He is continuing to work at home. He can make only 100 nails a day and he can only sell his product locally. The large nail factories might well put him out of business but he has the advantage of being his own boss and working at home.
* *Gradgrind the factory owner* His machines can produce large amounts of nails cheaply and efficiently. He employs a lot of people in his factory and probably only pays them a low wage. He can sell his nails wholesale at a good price to shop owners and building firms. He might even export them. The new railway system will greatly help his business (see sheet 5 *Railways*).
* *Factory worker* He has a job and probably brings home just enough for his family to live on. Whether this standard of living is better or worse than when he was his own boss is difficult to say. The conditions he has to work in are hard, as the list of rules on the wall indicates.

Extension activities

1 The children could produce a drama set in one of the new factories, perhaps Gradgrind's nail factory. Some children could be the workers on the production line, others child workers having to do the dangerous jobs such as climbing under the machines to clean them. The teacher or another child could take the part of factory owner. The factory owner decides to cut the workers' wages and step up the speed of production. What happens?
2 Groups could undertake further investigations into children working in factories. Then they could write the story of a day in the life of a factory child.

The factory system

Steam power meant that bigger machines could be used to make more things, more quickly. Things were made in factories, not in people's homes or in small workshops.

Write down whether you think the new factory system was a good or a bad thing for each of these people, and why.

3 Child labour

· ·

Skills

Using historical evidence
Making deductions from evidence
Reconstructing the past from evidence
Empathising with people in the past

Attainment targets

Level	AT1	AT2	AT3
2			✓
3			✓
4			✓
5			

Background information

Children were used in a variety of jobs during Victorian times. Many worked down the mines, in the mills and as chimney sweeps. Others were employed in domestic service, in brick and tile-making industries, as street sellers and as farm workers. In the 1840s enquiries were launched into the working conditions of children. As a result steps were taken to improve things. These included shorter working hours and a ban on the employment of very young children. The new laws were often ignored.

The following is an excerpt from the Mines Report of 1842. Sarah Gooder (aged 8) says of her job:

It does not tire me but I have to trap (opening and closing air-doors) *without a light and I am scared. I never go to sleep. Sometimes I sing when I've light, but not in the dark. I dare not sing then. I don't like being in the pit.*

Introductory work

The children might discuss the sorts of jobs children do today and at what age they are allowed to start part-time and full-time work. This could lead on to comparison with the sorts of jobs depicted on the sheet.

Using the sheet

There is quite a lot to discuss on the sheet before the children do the activity. Points to bring out include exactly what the children are doing in each picture, whether there are any dangers involved in the job, what the written evidence tells us about child labour and what else it tells us about life at that time.

The children are asked to write a report for Lord Shaftesbury. This could be written as if the child is an inspector, possibly a member of Lord Shaftesbury's team. The report might include illustrations and any further information the children can find out from books. Useful books include: *Victorian Children* by Eleanor Allen (A & C Black Ltd); *Victorian Childhood* by Pamela Harper (Batsford); *The Victorians* by Greg Thie (Basil Blackwell); *In Search of History* 1714-1900 (Edward Arnold) – particularly chapter 3 on mining.

Extension activities

1 To follow up the children's recommendations the teacher could give them details of some of the many laws passed as a result of Shaftesbury's enquiries. A GCSE textbook would be a good place to locate these.
2 Children could do further work on laws and rules, what laws are made for and how they are enforced. School rules are a good way in to this topic.
3 *Lark Rise to Candleford* by Flora Thompson (Chapter 10) describes how many girls entered domestic service at 10 or 11 years old. Children might research further into what domestic service entailed.
4 The class could conduct a parliamentary debate on child labour. One child could take the role of Lord Shaftesbury who makes a speech against child labour with one or two supporters. Two or three children could give the opposing view. Then the whole class could take a vote.

Child labour

Until 1870 British children did not have to go to school. Children from poor families had to go out to work. Below is some evidence about the jobs children did in Victorian times.

Lord Shaftesbury tried to get laws made to stop children having to do this work.

Children are taken into the mines to work as early as four years of age . . . eight or nine is the ordinary age at which work in these mines begins . . .

Advertisement
William Burgess — chimney sweep — has boys of the best size for a tunnel or a chimney. He carries them from room to room to keep soot off the floors . . .

Use the evidence on the sheet to write a report for Lord Shaftesbury. Write about the jobs children do and the places they work in. What law would you make to help the children?

4 Inventions

Skills

Using historical evidence
Making deductions from evidence
Identifying differences between past and present

Attainment targets

Level	AT1	AT2	AT3
2	√		√
3			√
4	√		
5			

Background information

The Great Exhibition was held in Hyde Park, London in 1851. It was an opportunity for British manufacturers to show off their goods and workmanship. Over six million people visited the exhibition.

The Crystal Palace was built especially to house the exhibition. It was made entirely from glass and iron, with a great curved roof so that trees growing on the site did not have to be cut down. Queen Victoria called it 'One of the wonders of the world!'

Introductory work

It would be useful if the children could have some experience of handling real objects before examining the ones shown on the sheet. Your county museum service or local museum may be able to lend you objects from Victorian times, or children in the class may have things they could bring in. As well as the questions on the sheet the following could be asked: How was it made? Was it made by hand or by machine? Is it well designed? What is it worth?
English Heritage have produced a book *Learning from Objects* which contains lots of ideas (address in resources section).

Using the sheet

There are clues in each picture to help the children guess what each object is. This might work well as a group activity, beginning with children 'brainstorming' possible uses. The labels could be written on card and then attached to cardboard cut-outs of the inventions to make a classroom exhibition.

Extension activities

1 Children could make a list of everyday objects in their own homes and consider what powers each of them. The absence of electricity in early Victorian times will soon become apparent. Children could imagine what a day without electricity would be like for them.
2 Lots more work can be done on using Victorian objects in the classroom eg create your own museum, try to match Victorian objects with the modern equivalent (the old flat iron with a modern iron), try to arrange a selection of objects in chronological order, discuss what clues objects give us about life in Victorian times.
3 Children could design a poster to advertise the Great Exhibition.
4 There were many other inventions in Victorian times. They include: gas burners (this had a huge impact on people's lives – for the first time they had an easy form of lighting in the home and on the streets), telephone, sewing machine, canned food, gramophone, typewriter, car (see sheet 6 *Cars*) and photography (see sheet 14 *Photography*). Children could make a list of these and then put them in order according to which they think the Victorians would have seen as most important.
5 The Crystal Palace was the winning entry of a competition to design a building for the Great Exhibition. What sort of building might the children design for such an exhibition today? Having designed a building, what exhibits would they put in to show off the best modern inventions?

Inventions

In 1851 the Great Exhibition was held in London. It had all the latest inventions. The exhibition was held inside a huge glass building nicknamed 'The Crystal Palace'.

CRYSTAL PALACE

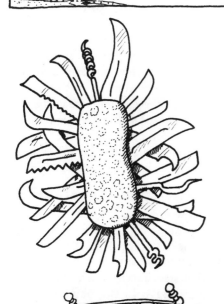

coffee

Here are four inventions that were on show at the Great Exhibition. Write a label for each one. Say:
* what you think it is
* how you think it works
* what powers it
* whether we use anything like this today.

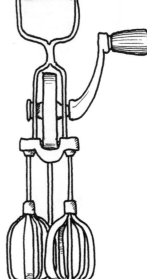

5 Railways

. . . .

Skills

Using historical evidence
Making deductions from evidence
Analysing change over a period of time
Identifying cause and consequence

Attainment targets

Level	AT1	AT2	AT3
2			
3	√		√
4	√		
5			

Background information

The first steam locomotive to run on rails was built in 1804. By 1830 the first passenger railway was opened. From then on the railways became a widespread and popular method of transport for both people and goods. The advantages of rail over coach travel or canal transportation were reliability, cheapness, safety and speed. As train services improved it became possible for ordinary people to go on holiday, especially to the seaside (see sheet 20 *Time off*). Railways had a huge impact on the economy. The coal and steel industries grew, creating new jobs and cheaper goods. Mail was transported by rail which in turn speeded up communication across the country.

Using the sheet

The children first have to work out the cost of the three rail prices. Using this information and the cost of the two coach fares they can draw a bar chart, with price on the vertical axis and rail and coach travel on the horizontal axis. The children should then be able to compare the costs. For the second activity the children need *Resource sheet* 2. Points to bring out are: the variety of places that could be reached by rail; impact of the rail network (holidays, faster journeys and communications); comparisons with rail travel today. *Note* The prices of the fares have been changed into modern currency.

Extension activities

1 The children could work out how long it would take to get from London to Birmingham by rail, using the map on *Resource sheet 2*. They could then work out how long it would take by stagecoach. To do this they need to work out how far it is by road from London to Birmingham, using a map, and know that stagecoaches travelled at approximately 10 miles an hour. Once they have the two times, does this affect their original choice of travel?

2 Children could design posters extolling the virtues of train travel. When the posters are displayed the class could discuss them. Are they biased? Do they contain facts or opinions? (This is good AT2 work.) An extension would be to design posters about rail travel from the stagecoach owners' point of view, ie putting forward the objections to rail travel.

3 Groups of children could role play representatives of rail and coach firms who try to persuade a group of passengers to travel by their particular means. What arguments could be used? What issues will be raised? Farmers whose land was taken over, canal workers, coach workers, innkeepers whose coach custom declined, could also be brought into the role play.

4 There are various railway museums which are worth a visit, or which may supply resources. These include the Railway Museum in York, Swindon Railway cottages and Didcot Railway Centre.

5 Famous figures connected with the railways include George Stephenson, Isambard Brunel and George Hudson. Groups could research a 'This is your life' for each man and present it to the rest of the class.

The first main line railway opened in 1830. The trains were pulled by steam locomotives. By 1850 railways linked most large towns and cities in Britain. Rail soon took over from road or canal transport.

BIRMINGHAM IN 3 HOURS. FARES   1st class = 4p a mile   2nd class = 2p a mile   3rd class = 1p a mile

STAGECOACH
London to Birmingham
FARES
Inside   4p a mile
Outside   2p a mile
Leave London   6.a.m
Arrive Birmingham   6 p.m.

You live in Victorian London and you want to travel to Birmingham, a distance of 110 miles. Work out how much it would cost you to travel by train, going 1st class, 2nd class or 3rd class. Draw a bar graph to compare rail prices with stagecoach prices. How would you choose to travel from London to Birmingham in Victorian times?

Use the map on Resource Sheet 2 and make a list of all the towns that you could get to from London by rail within four hours.

6 Cars

• •

Skills

Identifying differences between past and present
Identifying changes over a period of time

Attainment targets

Level	AT1	AT2	AT3
2	✓		
3	✓	✓	
4	✓		
5			

Background information

Motor cars or 'horseless carriages' were first seen in Britain in 1895. They were limited to a maximum speed of 6 kilometres an hour and had to be preceded by a man carrying a red flag. The speed limit was soon upped to 19km an hour as it was found that 6 km was just too slow! Queen Victoria did not like the new cars. She thought they 'smell exceedingly nasty and are very shaky and disagreeable.' Her son, Edward, was a very keen motorist.

Introductory work

Children could consider what came before the invention of the motor car and the impact it had on people then. Car makers used advertisements to persuade people of the advantages of the car over a horse-drawn carriage. One advert used as a reason 'It won't die or fall sick!' The children could discuss what some of the other advantages might be. What might the disadvantages be?

They could also imagine what it might have been like to see a car for the first time. Would they have been scared or excited by this new invention?

Using the sheet

After considering some of the advantages of cars over horse-drawn carriages children should be able to tackle the activity of writing a letter persuading Edward to buy one of the cars shown on the sheet. The children should also look closely at each of the cars to decide which might suit Edward best. He was a very fat gentleman, as the picture indicates.

Edward is shown wearing the essential clothes for motoring – why were these clothes needed?

Extension activities

1 Invite the children to imagine they are the 'Great Horseless Carriage Co Ltd'. They have to design a poster/advert encouraging people to buy a new car, the 'Twin-Cylinder 6HP Wagonette'.
2 Children could write a description of a modern car for someone in Victorian times to read.
3 Children could make a list of the differences there would be in our lives today if there were no motor cars. Ask the children to decide which they think would be the biggest difference.

Cars

One important invention during Queen Victoria's reign was the petrol-engined motor car. Victoria's son, Edward, was a very keen motorist.

goggles

gauntlets

dust coat

Motoring clothes

Jeantaud's cab 1896
Top speed 12 mph

Prince Edward wants to buy a new car. Write a letter to him telling him which car you think he should buy, and why.

Léon Bollée 1897
Top speed 25 mph

These cars look very different to modern ones. Can you find six differences?

Krieger 1898
Top speed 15 mph

De Dion Bouton 1899
Top speed 20 mph

Why do you think motorists wore these clothes?

7 The Trade of the Empire

Skills

Identifying cause and consequence

Attainment targets

Level	AT1	AT2	AT3
2			
3	✓		
4	✓		
5			

Background information

In Victorian times the British Empire was at its greatest. It included Canada, Australia, New Zealand, India, settlements in Africa and the Far East and islands in the Caribbean, the Pacific and Indian Oceans. The Victorians thought that Europe was the most civilised part of the world and that its role was to conquer and civilise the rest of the world.

Trade was a vital factor in Britain's hold over the Empire. A trade cycle existed: Britain would buy cheap, raw materials from abroad and then sell highly priced finished goods back to the countries of the Empire.

Introductory work

The notion of Empire will need to be introduced and talked about. This might begin by looking at a map of the world and identifying the Commonwealth countries, explaining that they are the remnants of the British Empire. The fact that English is so widely spoken around the world is a legacy of the Empire.

Using the sheet

The children will need a copy of *Resource sheet* 3 (a map of the Empire) to help them with the activity.

They should look at the products and discuss why they think they came from Empire countries and not from Britain (climate mainly). The words 'import' and 'export' will also need to be explained and discussed. They could be linked to imports and exports today.

Extension activities

1 The children could plot on the map of the Empire where all the imports and exports have come from and are going to. They might then work out how far the various goods have travelled and what route the ship might have taken. Another aspect to draw out would be the implications for price depending on how far the goods had travelled. To follow this theme further a group of children could take each country and do some research from secondary sources about what the country is like.

2 Children could make a 'trade' board game. The players could be trading companies visiting different countries, picking up goods on board their ship, coping with disasters on the way (eg pirates, disease on ship, products going bad) and making money as they sell the goods to manufacturers in Britain.

3 The problem of preserving goods on board ship for long journeys could be investigated further. What clues are there in the pictures on the activity sheet about packaging? Children might take tin cans for granted but one of the primary reasons this form of packaging was invented was as a means of preserving perishable goods.

4 Explorers such as Dr Livingstone (who travelled through Africa) had exciting adventures. Some of their stories will be interesting to children. They could also plot their explorers' journeys on a map.

The trade of the Empire

By 1880 British farms could not grow enough food to feed everyone. Food and other things were imported from all over the British Empire. Many of these were foods British people had never eaten before, like bananas. In return, things made in British factories were exported to countries in the Empire.

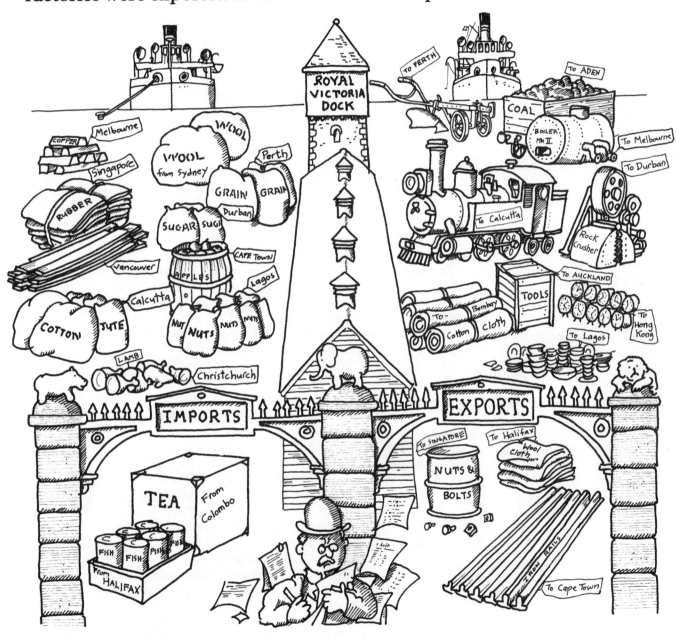

The dock manager has got his lists muddled up. Can you help him? Make a list of all the imports (things coming into Britain); make another list of all the exports (things going out of Britain). Look at the name of the port on each load. Use the map of the Empire on Resource Sheet 3 to find out which country the load has come from or is going to. Write the name of the country next to that load on your list.

8 The growth of towns

Skills

Identifying cause and consequence
Identifying changes over a period of time

Attainment targets

Level	AT1	AT2	AT3
2	√		
3	√		
4	√		
5			

Background information

Many factors contributed to the growth of towns in Victorian times. These include a growth in population, an improvement in communication systems (better roads, railways) and the expansion of new industries, particularly in the North of England. Many big industrial towns grew up without any planning and soon turned into polluted and unhealthy places to live and work (see Sheet 9 *Public health*).

Introductory work

Resource sheet 4 has a map showing how towns grew during Victorian times. Children could count up the number of large towns in 1851 and then 1901. The class could also discuss why they think particular towns grew, although they will need extra information to do this, such as the railway map (*Resource sheet 2*) areas of mining and textile industries.

Using the sheet

The children will need to consider each stage in the growth of the town – it is important that they understand that one advancement leads to another. What will be the impact of the coming of the railway line? Why do more houses need to be built?
There is no absolute correct order although the progression the children produce should make sense chronologically.

Extension activities

1 The children could compare the towns map with a map showing Britain's population today. Which big towns today were large towns in Victorian times? Have any of the Victorian towns become smaller? What do the children think is the reason for this? Are there any new big towns that were not there in Victorian times?
2 The children could create their own town on a large sheet of paper. The teacher starts it off as a small village with lots of blank space round it. Child 1 is a mill owner, and marks their mill on the paper. Child 2 represents 50 workers and draws in their houses. Child 3 is a factory owner – where do they put their factory? And so on.
   When they have all finished, encourage the children to stand back and look at their town. What is wrong with it? The drawing is likely to be a muddle, with factories too close to houses and no room for certain essentials. The point is to show that many of the problems in Victorian towns were caused by lack of planning.
   The children could start again with a new town, this time thinking about planning, eg there must be some open space, houses should be well away from factories . . .
3 Census returns (produced every 10 years since 1801) are a good indication of population growth and the development of new housing areas. Interesting comparison work could be done if the teacher can get hold of census returns for, say, 1841 and 1891. Your local library/record office should have the census on microfiche.

The growth of towns

Many Victorian towns grew very fast. There were many reasons why towns got bigger. The pictures below show how one particular town grew. But the pictures are muddled up. Cut the pictures out and put them in the right order.

Shops and churches are built

Coal is discovered

A factory is built, with steam-powered machinery

More factories built because goods can be moved quickly by rail

A railway line is built

The town becomes a large industrial city

A small and sleepy country town

More people come to work in the factory

More people come Hundreds of new houses are built

People come to mine the coal

Look at the map on Resource Sheet 4 to find out more about Victorian towns.

9 Public health

Skills

Using historical evidence
Making deductions from evidence
Identifying different types of cause and consequence
Empathising with people of the past

Attainment targets

Level	AT1	AT2	AT3
2			✓
3	✓		✓
4	✓		✓
5			

Background information

The growth of industry and the expansion of towns and cities was followed by bad living conditions and disease. Cheaply built, back-to-back terraced houses were hastily put up to house families who had come to the towns looking for work. Ventilation and lighting were poor, water had to be collected from a street tap or local river, outside toilets were shared by many families.

Between 1848 and 1875 several public health laws were passed. This eventually resulted in a reduction in the number of deaths from diseases such as cholera and typhoid and better conditions in streets and homes.

Introductory work

The teacher might begin by reading and discussing the quote below. In 1832 a Dr Kay wrote about Manchester:

The houses are ill-drained, often ill-ventilated, unprovided with toilets and in consequence, the streets which are narrow, unpaved and worn into deep ruts, become the common resting place of mud, refuse and disgusting rubbish . . . In Parliament Street there is only one toilet for 380 inhabitants, which is placed in a narrow passage, from where its flow of muck infests the close-by houses, and must prove a most fertile source of disease.

It would also be useful to get hold of photographs/line drawings/ engravings depicting Victorian street life to discuss with the children. Your local studies library may contain some examples from your own town.

Using the sheet

This sheet leads on quite well from sheet 8 *Growth of towns* – the town depicted on this sheet was the result of the growth of towns. Children will need *Resource sheet 5* to read through the public health regulations. This might usefully be done as a whole class, with discussion about what the regulations mean and why they were necessary. The resource sheet also provides a table for the children to fill in.

Extension activities

1 Infringements of the public health laws can be extended into role-play/drama. Children could act out a trial scene, in which the defendant has broken one of the laws and has to argue their case against the prosecution.
2 Children could imagine what it might have been like to visit, say Manchester, in Victorian times and to go around a cotton worker's house. They could describe what they might have seen, heard and smelt and what they might have felt like. The quote in *Background information* and further information from reference books would help with this activity.
3 Children could list differences between the town depicted on the sheet and their town (or nearest town) today. They might discuss why things have changed so much. Can they find any similarities? Many children live in Victorian workers' terraced houses today. Some of the workers' estates have developed into quite expensive housing areas.

Public health

Many large towns in Victorian Britain were unhealthy and polluted places.

Read the public health laws on Resource Sheet 5 and decide how this town is breaking the rules.

10 Education

Skills

Using historical evidence
Identifying similarities and differences between past and present

Attainment targets

Level	AT1	AT2	AT3
2	✓		✓
3			✓
4	✓		✓
5			

Background information

Before 1870 most poor children started work very young and did not go to school at all. Some schools existed, including church schools and dame schools, but they were very grim and lacked even basic resources. Parents had to pay for their children to attend.

The Eduation Act of 1870 began a series of reforms which initiated the setting up of school boards, the building of new schools and laws requiring all children between the ages of 5 and 13 to go to school. Middle and upper class parents sent their children to fee-paying grammar, public and private schools.

The following books contain further information about Victorian schools, including both primary and secondary source material: *Finding out about Victorian Childhood* P Harper (Batsford); *Into the Past: At School in 1900* S Purkiss (Longman); *Victorian Children* E Allen (A and C Black); *Finding out about Victorian Schools* A Clarke (Batsford).

Introductory work

Chapters 11/12 of *Lark Rise to Candleford* by Flora Thompson contain some of the author's memories of going to school in the 1880s. The teacher might like to set the scene by reading a section from the book to the children. Ask the children to write down or remember any words or phrases that they don't understand, eg the '3R's, pinafores, hob-nailed boots, dunce, cane, scripture. Compile a class list and then the children can try to find out what each of the things is.

Using the sheet

Encourage the children to discuss the picture first, possibly picking a few things that they can see in the picture that they find interesting. They should easily find eight differences, probably more. As well as the more obvious things, the teacher might draw the children's attention to things such as the windows, walls, number of pupils, the layout of the classroom, names of some of the lessons.

Extension activities

1 Re-enact a day in a Victorian classroom with children and teachers in costume, Victorian lessons, punishments and discipline, PE or drill, as it was known – even a Victorian lunch!

2 Children could compare discipline and rules in Victorian schools with rules today. Do they think the rules were fair? Why do they think the Victorians had such strict discipline?

3 One of the crafts practised in a Victorian classroom was making a sampler. Children could make their own samplers which might include the alphabet, the name and age of the child, a text from the Bible or a saying and a border.

4 Children might compare the sort of school depicted on the sheet with a typical boarding school of the time. *Nicholas Nickleby* by Charles Dickens and *Tom Brown's Schooldays* by Thomas Hughes gives evidence for this.

Education

In 1870 a new law said that all children had to go to school. The picture shows a classroom in 1880.

List eight differences between this classroom and your own classroom. Are any things the same?

11 Religion

Skills

Analysing facts and points of view

Attainment targets

Level	AT1	AT2	AT3
2 3 4 5		✓	

Background information

Religion was a very important part of Victorian life and beliefs. Religious Victorians were almost all Christians, comprising many different groups – Roman Catholics, Church of England, Methodists, Quakers, Baptists and Evangelicals, for example. Existing churches were extensively restored during Victorian times and many new churches were built. Religious families kept Sunday strictly as a day of rest and prayer, many families going to church several times during the day. All the shops were closed and there was no sport or amusement. *A Victorian Sunday* by J Hughes (Wayland) gives further information.

Introductory work

Begin by discussing with the children what they do on a Sunday, perhaps asking a few children to describe a typical day. Then read out an account of a typical Sunday for a child in Victorian times. Chapter 14 of Flora Thompson's *Lark Rise to Candleford* is entitled 'To church on Sunday' and contains a lot of information about religion. Chapter 4 of *David Copperfield* by Charles Dickens has a section about David's experiences at church.

Using the sheet

The children should read through the whole day, then list all the different things said by the characters in the story. It might be useful to discuss with the children what a *fact* and a *point of view* are, and how they differ. Children could be asked for modern examples, eg 'It's lunchtime' is a fact, but 'I love school dinners' a point of view, what someone thinks. After discussing a few examples they should be able to do the ones in the story on the sheet.

Extension activities

1 The Sunday portrayed on the sheet can be compared with a modern Sunday. What has changed? What has stayed the same?
2 Children might write a diary entry for the Victorian Sunday, from the point of view of the child or of the mother. Comparing the two different accounts would be useful AT2 work – the two people have followed the same day so why are the accounts so different?
3 Almost all religious Victorians were Christians. Sunday was the day they went to Church. The teacher might ask how many children in the class go to some sort of religious gathering. Where do they go? On what day? Children could be invited to tell the class about what they do and what religion they practise.

30

Religion

Religion was an important part of Victorian life. Most religious people in Victorian Britain were Christians. They said Sunday was the Lord's Day. They went to church and were serious and solemn on Sundays.

Make a list of what each person says about the Victorian Sunday. Which of them are **facts** and which are **points of view?**

12 Medical improvements

Teacher's notes

∙∙

Skills

Identifying and describing changes over a period of time
Identifying cause and consequence

Attainment targets

Level	AT1	AT2	AT3
2	√		
3			
4	√		
5			

Background information

By the end of the 19th century everyone except the very poor could expect a longer, healthier life. Many significant advances were made in medicine as well as general improvements in public health. Antiseptics and anaesthetics improved surgery; vaccines were developed for killer diseases such as smallpox; this saved many lives. Hospitals were also improving, as was the standard of nursing (mainly due to the efforts of Florence Nightingale). Medical treatment was not free – an operation or treatment by a doctor had to be paid for, although a few dedicated doctors charged high fees to the rich so that they could treat the poor almost free of charge.

Introductory work

The children might discuss what happens today when someone goes into hospital to have an operation. A comparison can then be made with Victorian times when they come to do the activity on the sheet.

Using the sheet

Before listing all the differences between the two operations the children should look carefully to see exactly what is going on in each picture. The main differences to be brought out are:
- the use of carbolic spray to combat infection
- the patient being anaesthetised
- better care being taken of the operating instruments
- much cleaner conditions
- no sawdust on the floor to absorb the blood!
- the presence of a nurse at the operation
- women students watching the later operation

After spotting the differences the children could think about what the advantages of all these improvements were.

Extension activities

1 Further investigation could be done on Florence Nightingale and her work both in the Crimean War and at home. Reference books about Florence Nightingale include: *Florence Nightingale* (Wayland' Great Lives' series) *Florence Nightingale* (Franklin Watts' 'Lifetimes' series)
2 Before the introduction of mass-produced pills and medicines doctors used 'cures' that might seem very strange to us today in Britain. The *Medical Almanac* for 1856 advises as a cure for apoplexy (fits):
… leeches to the temple, one or two drops of croton oil rubbed or dropped on the tongue … Take powdered rhubarb and chloride of mercury each four grains …
Can the children think of any unusual cures or remedies people use to treat illness today?

32

Medical improvements

At the beginning of Victoria's reign having an operation was painful and dangerous. Many patients died during their operation; others died later, from infections.

Joseph Lister was a surgeon. He found out that germs caused infections. He used antiseptics to kill the germs. Doctors found they could use chloroform as an anaesthetic. This sent patients to sleep, so that they did not feel the pain of the operation.

Look at the two pictures of an operation, one in 1840 and the other in 1890. Imagine you were one of the students in 1840. You have come back to watch the 1890 operation. Write down all the differences between the two operations.

13 Buildings

Teacher's notes

Skills

Using historical evidence
Analysing different elements of historical style

Attainment targets

Level	AT1	AT2	AT3
2			
3			✓
4	✓		✓
5			

Background information

Victorian architects used a variety of styles, imitating many features from the past. These ranged from 'Classical' columns and pediments to a craze for 'Gothic' buildings, with gables, turrets and ornamental stonework. Everyday buildings such as schools, public houses and churches were subject to this variety of style. So were some famous public buildings of the time, eg The Ashmolean Museum in Oxford, Birmingham Cathedral, the Houses of Parliament, St. Pancras station, the Town Halls of Leeds and Halifax.

Architects of note were Charles Barry (Houses of Parliament), Charles Cockerell (Ashmolean Museum), Augustus Pugin (Birmingham Cathedral) Joseph Paxton (The Crystal Palace) and Sir George Gilbert Scott (Albert Memorial).

Introductory work

An explanation of the various different architectural styles would help the children when they come to look at the buildings on the sheet. *Resource sheet 6* shows examples of Victorian architecture.

If your school is in or near a town with Victorian buildings it would be useful to visit them and talk about the various styles that can be seen.

Using the sheet

The children will need to look closely at the various buildings on the sheet to find the different styles and shapes of windows and doors. Alternatively the teacher could give out a sheet with the different styles already drawn, for the children to 'Spot the style'. They could present their own drawings as an architectural catalogue with different categories. If they have a reference book to help them, they might describe the different styles in writing and some children might be able to identify and name the particular architectural styles.

Extension activities

1 The children could draw and cut out a family who might live in their personally-designed house. The family could be put 'inside' the house, either up on the wall or in their topic books/folders.
2 Children could compare the styles of windows and doors used on buildings today with those found on Victorian buildings. They could discuss what they like or dislike about the various styles.
3 Children could make 'junk' models of some famous Victorian buildings.

Buildings

Thousands of new buildings were put up in the growing towns and cities. The Victorians did not stick to just one style of building. They tried many different ones.

The pictures show some buildings that this architect has designed. Draw your own house using the different styles of windows and chimneys on Resource Sheet 6.

14 Photography

Skills

Analysing different viewpoints about the past
Analysing changes over a period of time

Attainment targets

Level	AT1	AT2	AT3
2 3 4 5	√	√	

Background information

The earliest photographic advances were made by a Frenchman, Joseph Niepce who produced the first fixed image on a chemically-coated plate. The first British person connected with the invention of the photographic process was William Fox Talbot. He produced the first print from a negative in 1835 which meant that any number of prints could be made from the same shot. Roll film was introduced in 1885; this speeded up the process of taking photos. Cameras remained large and cumbersome – it wasn't until well into the 20th century that the first hand-held cameras were seen.

Introductory work

The teacher could arrange a group as if for a photograph, and ask them to sit upright and very still for about 40 seconds – the time it would take to take a photograph in early Victorian times!
As well as the sitting time it took a lot of time to prepare the camera, take the plate out afterwards and then develop the picture. The children could compare this with what is involved in taking a photograph today.

Using the sheet

The arguments on the sheet really did take place in Victorian times. Two children could take on the roles of the photographer and painter and read out the arguments as if they really are having an argument. The meaning of some of the arguments will need to be discussed, eg 'The camera never lies' – do the children agree with this? 'Paintings can be in colour' – what does this tell us about photography in Victorian times?

The class could compare their choices of 'persuasive' arguments – Are they all the same? The children could also sort the arguments into *facts* and *opinions*.

Extension activities

1 Children could make a cartoon flick book. Each page of the book shows a figure running or walking in a slightly different position. When the book is flicked through the figure appears to be moving! Cartoons also work on this principle.
2 Victorian photographs are an excellent source of evidence about Victorian times and are widely available in reference books, local studies libraries and museums, and from local history societies.
   If the teacher can get hold of Victorian photos of the local area, children could go out and take a modern photo of the same place. They can then do useful comparision work on what has changed and what has stayed the same.
3 Silhouette portraits were very popular in Victorian times, being cheaper than photography or painting. Children could make their own silhouettes by shining a bright light against a sheet of paper on the wall with the subject in between. Another child could draw around the shadow to form the silhouette image.
4 The National Museum of Photography and Film in Bradford is a useful place to visit. You could write to them for information about the history of photography.

Photography

During Queen Victoria's reign photography was invented. Some painters were very worried that photography would put them out of a job. People argued about which was best: painting or photography.

It's more realistic. You can get an exact likeness. It's much cheaper. It only takes a few minutes to take a photograph. You don't have to be able to draw to make a life-like picture. It's more honest. The camera never lies.

Paintings can be in colour. Paintings can be as big as you like. You can make people better looking than they really are. You can use your imagination to make pictures of things that don't exist, or you can paint something after it has happened. There is only one of any painting – that makes it more valuable. It takes more skill to make a painting.

Which do you think are the **two** best arguments for photography? Which are the **two** best arguments for painting?

Imagine you are a Victorian painter or photographer. Write an advertisement for yourself, using these arguments.

Skills

Using historical evidence
Empathising with people in the past

Attainment targets

Level	AT1	AT2	AT3
2	√		√
3	√		
4			
5			

Background information

Many 'classic' Victorian novels were originally published in serial form in literary magazines. The work of authors like Charles Dickens would be read aloud, providing an exciting evening's entertainment for the whole family – especially as each episode usually ended with a 'cliff-hanger.'

Other authors of the times whose books are now considered children's classics include Lewis Caroll (*Alice in Wonderland*), Robert Louis Stephenson (*Treasure Island*), Charles Kingsley (*The Water Babies*) and Anna Sewell (*Black Beauty*).

Introductory work

Bring in a selection of novels written in Victorian times and read out a few extracts. The class could discuss the idea of a literary magazine and how novels were first serialised in these. Some children's magazines contain serialised stories – children might be able to bring in examples.
Children will be familiar with the idea of a serial from watching television, particularly soap operas. The technique of finishing at a critical point provides the hook to make you watch next time. Victorian literary magazines worked in a very similar way.

Using the sheet

After reading the information on the sheet the class could discuss where they think four episodes of *The Old Curiosity Shop* could start and stop. They could mark this on the sheet or cut the pictures out and group them. The class should then split into four groups, each taking an episode. Each group works out what happens in their section of the story and writes their episode as a group writing exercise.

The whole class can decide whether Little Nell dies or not and what happens in the end. This can then be compared with what happens in the real story!

The picture of the boat being met by the the crowds can be discussed. What does it tell us about Dickens' popularity? How might serial magazines be delivered today to America? By plane? By fax?

Extension activities

1 Compare a Victorian evening's entertainment listening to Father reading a novel to evening entertainment today. What are the differences? Why has it changed so much?

2 Children's comics were also produced in Victorian times, eg *Little Folks*, *Girls' Own Paper*. The stories often contained a moral message and were thought good for young Christian minds. Children could produce their own Victorian comics with stories based on real novels of the time or their own stories, along with advertisements for the latest toys (see sheet 19 *Toys*), pictures to colour in etc.

3 Children could use extracts from literature about Victorian times to build up a picture of particular aspects of life, eg street children from *Oliver Twist*, chimney sweeps from *The Water Babies*, school life from *Lark Rise to Candleford*. Clothes children wore can be discovered from illustrations in books such as *Alice in Wonderland*.

Literature

The Victorians read a lot. New printing presses could make many cheap books. More children were going to school and learning to read.

Queen Victoria was very fond of books. She even made an actress 'Reader to the Queen'. Her job was to read aloud to Victoria last thing at night, as she lay in bed.

Charles Dickens wrote many of his novels for a weekly magazine. He wrote them in episodes. Each episode had to end in an exciting way, to make sure the reader would buy the next magazine to find out what happened.

The suspense was so great that when the ship carrying the latest episode arrived in New York, it was met by crowds of people asking,

IS LITTLE NELL DEAD?

....

Skills

Using historical evidence
Making deductions from evidence

Attainment targets

Level	AT1	AT2	AT3
2			✓
3			✓
4			✓
5			

Background information

Victorian families were much larger than those of today. It was common to have eight to ten children. Fathers tended not to spend very much time with their children; they expected to be treated with great respect. They would remain slightly aloof and make all the important family decisions. Women had far less influence but they would often work twice as hard, clothing and feeding the family and looking after the house. Many women died in childbirth.

Children often died young – poor sanitation, inadequate diet and the lack of drugs to treat infection and disease caused a high child mortality rate. Tuberculosis, polio and measles were usually fatal.

Introductory work

What is the average family size of children in the class? What jobs do mothers and fathers do? Who makes important family decisions? How do children behave in the house? Who looks after the children when they are young? (This might be a sensitive area so the teacher should be aware of any questions that might be difficult for particular children.)
How could the children find out more about Victorian families? Where would they look to find information? What primary evidence might they use? As well as gravestones, information can be found in photographs, pictures and paintings, fiction of the time or diary entries, census returns (from your local studies library), and parish records of baptisms, marriages and burials from the parish church.

Using the sheet

The children will need to study the evidence on the gravestone to find out the answers to the questions. Each of the questions involves some deduction work and would benefit from discussion.

Extension activities

1 Question 5 on children's names could be extended into a survey of first names in the school. These could then be compared with common Victorian names. Census returns would be an excellent source of evidence for the Victorian names. Your local library or record office should have census returns for your area, taken every 10 years since 1801.
2 Further census work could involve investigating size of families and the occupations of family members.
3 The local graveyard can be a mine of information. *Resource sheet 7* is a graveyard census form for children to use. The children could also map the graveyard. The data collected can be sorted, classified and displayed in various ways using a data–handling computer programme.
4 The Obadiah Shovel family tree can be produced from the information shown on the sheet.
5 Children can compare old family photographs etc.
6 The children might imagine living in their present house with possibly seven or eight brothers and sisters. What changes would you have to make to your present lifestyle?

Victorian families

You can learn a lot from gravestones and memorials. This is my great-grandfather's.

SACRED TO THE
MEMORY
OF
The Revd. Obadiah Thomas
Adolphus SHOVEL MA. DD.
Born 1818 ~ passed to glory ~ 1899
Also Hannah his wife
1825 ~ 1850
and child Alice 1850 ~ 1852

And his wife Emily 1830 ~ 1910
and child George ~ 1861
This monument erected by
his grieving children
Henry Harriet Sarah Clara
Frederick Lucy John
and
His grateful parishioners at
All Saints - Pimlico where for
50 years he ministered.

Work out the answers to the following questions:

1 How old was Obadiah Shovel when he died?

2 What was his job?

3 How many times was he married?

4 What do you think happened to his first wife Hannah?

5 Look at the names of his children. Are they similar or different to children's names today?

17 Servants

Teacher's notes

•••

Skills

Making deductions from evidence

Attainment targets

Level	AT1	AT2	AT3
2			
3			✓
4			✓
5			

Background information

Servants formed an essential part of middle-and upper class Victorian households. Even families earning only £300 a year were recommended by Mrs Beeton in her *Book of Household Management* to have at least one general servant.

Servants would usually live 'downstairs' and sleep in the attics. Servants were often badly paid. A housemaid might expect to earn around £12, a cook £15 and a governess £20 a year. However food, clothing and lodging would be paid for and loyal servants might expect a good standard of living. Servants would often stay with the same family all their working life. Chapter 10 of *Lark Rise to Candleford* tells of girls from Lark Rise who went into service.

Introductory work

It would be useful to discuss exactly what a servant was. Children might have come across the notion of slaves in previous topics. It should be made clear that ownership of slaves is quite different from employing servants, although in some ways servants were financially bound to their masters and mistresses in Victorian times. Children may know that some families today employ 'servants', particularly cooks, nannies, gardeners and cleaners, some of whom live in.

Using the sheet

The pictures of each servant should give clues as to which job they did, and the children can use a reference book to help them. The order of importance may be difficult if the children have no previous knowledge. This might be best done as a class discussion. The clothes the servants wore give some clues as to their ranking in the household.

Extension activities

1 Children could choose one of the servants, eg housemaid, and write an advertisement for their job.
2 Groups could do further investigation into the different jobs each of the servants did. The children might write an account of a day in the life of, say, the butler in a busy London household. Or they could compose a diary entry for one of the kitchenmaids, including her feelings about the job and being a servant.
3 The class could hold a balloon debate: the family is getting poorer so one of the servants has to go. Children represent the servants and have to plead their case, saying why they are necessary.
4 Housemaids and kitchenmaids wore mob caps. These are easy to make. Cut out a circle of white material about 35cm across. Make an inner circle of stitching which can be pulled so that it fits around a child's head. These are useful if the class is going to re-enact a Victorian day!
5 Visits to Victorian stately homes give some clues about the sorts of jobs servants had to do, eg polishing the silver, dusting, making all the beds, cooking for great numbers of people who might come for banquets.

Servants

Most well-off families had at least one servant. Rich families had many more. The Prince of Wales had 88 servants to work in one house!

Most servants were girls and women. By 1890 over two and a half million worked as servants.

Butler Bootboy Coachman Cook Footman Gardener

Gardener's boy Groom Housekeeper Housemaid Kitchenmaid

Lady's maid Nurse Parlourmaid Scullerymaid Undergardener Valet

Work out which of these servants is which.
What sort of job did each of them do?
Put the jobs in order of importance, with the most important job at the top of the list, and the least important at the bottom.

18 Houses

Teacher's notes

Skills

Using historical evidence
Making deductions from evidence
Contrasting different aspects of housing in the past

Attainment targets

Level	AT1	AT2	AT3
2	√		√
3			√
4	√		√
5			

Background information

The middle and upper classes in Victorian times enjoyed a good standard of living in large two- or three-storied houses, often designed by architects to individual requirements. They were lavishly decorated and filled with the heavy dark furniture typical of Victorian style. It was fashionable to have many ornaments and pictures, filling and cluttering the rooms. These houses had the new luxuries of gas and water on tap, and indoor toilets. They were heated by coal. The description at the bottom of the sheet gives some clues to the conditions rural poor people lived in. Sheet 9 on *Public health* looks at the state of the urban poor.

Introductory work

The contrast between the way the different classes lived in Victorian times would be a useful way in to this topic. If your local town has Victorian housing the children could look at and compare the buildings themselves. Modern estate agents' reports on these contrasting types of houses will help bring the houses 'into the classroom', especially if they have photographs on them.
Chapter 1 of *Lark Rise to Candleford* by Flora Thompson describes living conditions for poor people in the countryside.

Using the sheet

The children should discuss the house on the sheet and try and work out what each of the rooms was used for. Some of them may be unfamiliar, eg the coal store, the cellar, the servants' attic bedroom. A good reference book will help them.
The teacher will also need to give the children some modern estate agents' 'blurbs' as examples of the style to use when they report on the Victorian house. The children can consider what the selling points of the house might be and even use the typical estate agents' language.

Extension activities

1 Contrast the house on the sheet with a similar modern house What rooms do we have today? Which don't we have?
2 Encourage the children to contrast the written details of the poor person's house with the drawn details of the rich house. They could draw a picture of the cottage.
3 Invite children to write a letter describing their experiences as if they were either a rich Victorian child visiting a poor cottage, or a poor child in a wealthy home.
4 Tiles were very popular in rich homes: in bathrooms, in hallways, inlaid on sideboards and fireplaces. Children could investigate the sort of designs used and make an inlaid tile of their own. They need a slab of clay (approx 15 cm by 15 cm) and tools to make a pattern which is then filled with coloured slip and fired.

44

Houses

Rich people in Victorian times had big and comfortable houses.

The house in the picture cost £200 to build, a lot of money then.

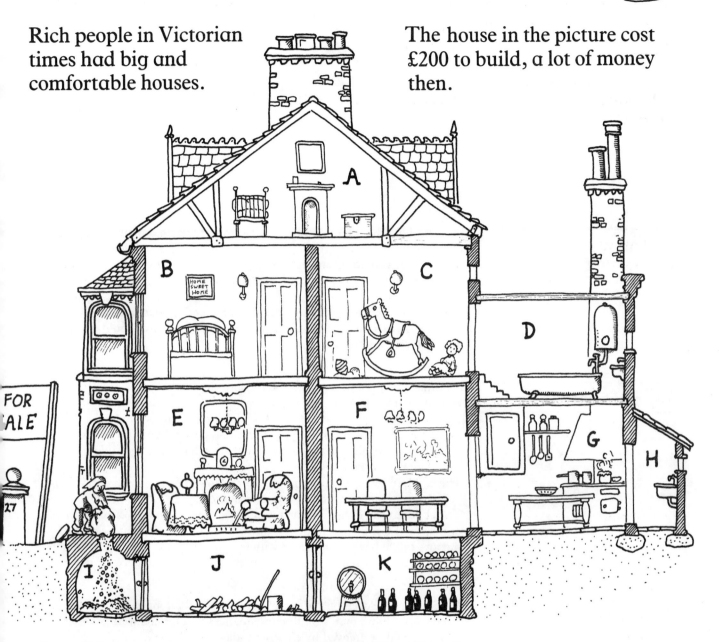

Not all homes were as comfortable as this. Here is a description of a poor person's cottage:

> The walls are made of straw, mixed with mud. The earth of the floor is full of vegetable matter. It is very damp. There are only three rooms. The roof is of thatch, which rots and gives off a gas that injures health.

The house in the picture is for sale! You are a Victorian estate agent. First invent a name for yourself, then write a report on the house to send out to interested buyers. Include information on all the rooms in the house and what they are used for.

19 Toys

Skills

Using historical evidence

Attainment targets

Level	AT1	AT2	AT3
2	✓		✓
3	✓		✓
4	✓		✓
5			

Background information

In Victorian times children played with toys or invented their own games. Outdoor games such as marbles, skipping and playing with hoops and spinning tops could be enjoyed by all children, the more elaborate toys like dolls' houses, rocking horses and train sets could only be afforded by the rich.

Victorian children by E Allen (A and C Black) and *How we used to live 1851-1901* (Macdonald) contain information and pictures about a whole range of Victorian toys.

Using the sheet

A number of questions can be asked about the toys: What is each toy? How does it work? Which of these toys do children still play with today? Which are not played with at all? Why don't children today play with toys like these? Would you like to play with these toys? Choose three of these toys that you would like to play with and say why. What age children would play with these toys?

The children might also discuss the sort of toys they play with today and how these are different to the toys on the sheet.

The children can either cut the toys out and sort them into the categories or make a list of them and then redraw them for the catalogue. Some of the toys might have been played with by both girls and boys, eg hoop, puppet – the children might wish to make a separate category for these.

Extension activities

1 Victorian children played many other games. Parlour games such as charades, blind man's bluff, consequences and forfeits were popular and would be enjoyed by children today.
2 Dolls were a great favourite with girls. Rich girls would own beautiful wax and china dolls dressed in gorgeous clothes, sometimes with real human hair. Poorer children would play with rag dolls (often just made from a wooden spoon and a piece of cloth) or peg dolls. Children could make peg dolls from the old style dolly pegs and pipe cleaners and dress them in Victorian outfits.
3 Children could make a thaumatrope, a popular Victorian spinning toy. A thaumatrope is a spinning disc with a picture on each side, eg a parrot on one side and a cage on the other. When the card is spun the parrot appears inside the cage!
4 Older children might have a model theatre. Children could make their own theatres with scenary and card figures moved about on the end of a stick. They could make up their own Victorian melodrama to act out.

Toys

Toys became very popular in Victorian times. Children from rich families had many toys to play with. Poorer children might have had only one or two toys.

You are opening a Victorian toy shop. Make a catalogue of all these toys. The catalogue should have four sections:

Indoor toys – girls **Outdoor toys – girls**
Indoor toys – boys **Outdoor toys – boys**

You can cut out the toys on this page to put in your catalogue.

20 Time Off

Skills

Using historical evidence
Making deductions from evidence
Identifying similarities and differences between past and present
Empathising with people of the past

Attainment targets

Level	AT1	AT2	AT3
2			✓
3			✓
4			✓
5			

Background information

Easy travel by train and the establishment of Bank holidays in 1871 gave many people the opportunity to enjoy holidays at the seaside. Seaside towns such as Brighton and Blackpool began to attract visitors in their thousands. Boarding houses, piers, promenades and other amusements were built to accommodate the holiday makers.

In the early years men and women used separate parts of the beach although this soon became more relaxed, as *The Observer* reported in 1865: *The portion of the beach allotted to the men is crowded with well-dressed females who look on without a blush or a giggle!*

Introductory work

The drawing on the sheet is based on a cartoon from the Victorian magazine *Fun*. *Victorian Children* By E Allen (A & C Black) contains pictorial and written evidence.

Using the sheet

Invite the children to discuss what a holiday at the seaside is like now. The first activity asks the children to find differences between the Victorian beach scene and a modern scene. After each child or group has found five differences the class might pool its findings and come up with a huge class list. They could also list the similarities.

To be able to do the second activity there will need to be some discussion as to what purpose the bathing machines served. Having established that they were to get changed in, the whole question of modesty and morality can be brought up.

Extension activities

1 The children could choose the five most interesting people in the picture and describe what they are doing. This can be shared as a class.
2 The children could imagine they are spending a day at the seaside in Victorian times and make a postcard to send to a friend. The postcard could show a seaside view with writing on the back.
3 As well as holidaymakers the beaches were crowded with people selling food, drinks and sourvenirs. Children could make up calls that the sellers might shout out as they try to sell their wares.
4 A seaside scene is a wonderful subject for a collage for the classroom wall. Each child could take a different part to make up in material or coloured paper.
5 'Time off' for the Victorians also included sporting activities, visits to sporting events, evenings at the music hall. Children could research and compile a Victorian entertainments guide.
6 Frith, whose scene is shown on the sheet, also portrayed a number of other crowd scenes, including one of Derby Day and one at Paddington Station which provide excellent evidence about life in Victorian times.

Time off

Seaside holidays were very popular in Victorian times. Queen Victoria had a family holiday home called Osborne House, on the Isle of Wight.

This picture shows a beach in 1865. What would a modern beach look like? Can you find five differences?

These are bathing machines. People hired them on the beach. Why do you think they used bathing machines? Write an advertisement to get people to hire your machines.

A Family Tree

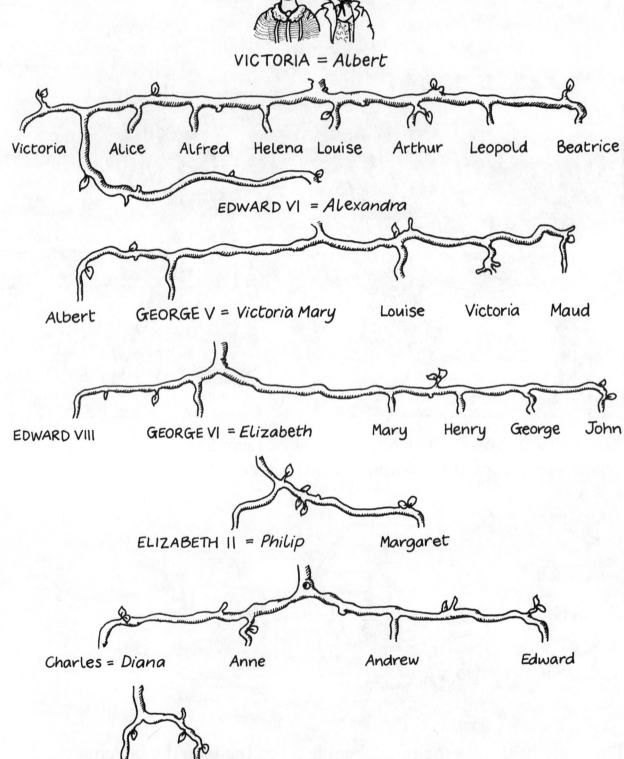

VICTORIA = Albert

Victoria   Alice   Alfred   Helena   Louise   Arthur   Leopold   Beatrice

EDWARD VI = Alexandra

Albert   GEORGE V = Victoria Mary   Louise   Victoria   Maud

EDWARD VIII   GEORGE VI = Elizabeth   Mary   Henry   George   John

ELIZABETH II = Philip   Margaret

Charles = Diana   Anne   Andrew   Edward

Henry   William

Resource Sheet 2

Train journey times from London

Legend:

- ⋯⋯ Under 1 hour
- ----- 2 hours
- ×××× 3 hours
- -··-··- 4 hours
- ∿∿∿∿ 5 hours
- -ı-ı-ı-ı 6 hours
- ∘∘∘∘ 7 hours
- ▬▬▬ Over 8 hours

The Empire and trade

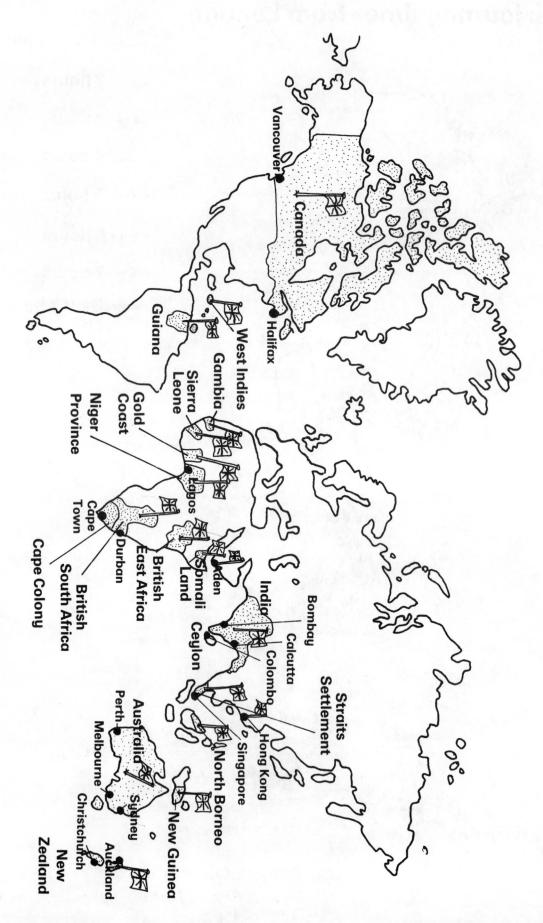

Resource Sheet 4

The growth of towns

Aberdeen

Dundee

Edinburgh

Glasgow

Newcastle
Gateshead
Sunderland
Middlesbrough

Bradford
Leeds
Huddersfield
Blackburn
Preston   Halifax   Hull
St Helens   Bolton
Liverpool   Oldham
Salford   Sheffield
Manchester   Stockport
Stoke   Nottingham
Derby   Norwich
                 Leicester
Birmingham

Cardiff

London

Bristol

Brighton
Southampton
Portsmouth
Plymouth

▨ **Towns with over 100,000 people in 1851**
⊙ **Towns with over 100,000 people in 1901**

© Fiona Goodman and Peter Kent. Simon & Schuster Education 1992

Resource Sheet 5

Public health

Public Health Act

1 All fireplaces or furnaces must be built as to consume all smoke arising from them.

2 No cows or pigs to be kept near houses.

3 No industrial waste or sewage to be dumped in the river.

4 All houses to be connected to a sewer.

5 All houses to have piped fresh water.

6 No rubbish to be thrown into the street.

7 All streets to be paved and at least 36 feet wide.

8 Every house to have a front and back door and enough windows for light and air.

9 No offensive trade or industry to be close to houses.

10 The Council must provide parks, public baths and burial grounds.

What is wrong?	What law is being broken?	Your suggested improvements

1 _____

2 _____

3 _____

4 _____

5 _____

6 _____

7 _____

8 _____

9 _____

10 _____

11 _____

12 _____

13 _____

14 _____

15 _____

16 _____

17 _____

18 _____

19 _____

20 _____

Victorian Style

Doors

Porches

Windows

Chimneys

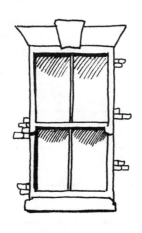

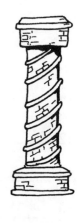

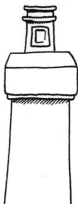

© Fiona Goodman and Peter Kent. Simon & Schuster Education 1992

Resource Sheet 7

Graveyard census at _____

Name _____   Sheet number _____

Grave number	Name	Sex	Age	Cause of death (if given)
1				
2				
3				
4				
5				
6				
7				
8				
9				
10				
11				
12				
13				
14				
15				
16				
17				
18				
19				
20				